SEEDS OF AWAKENING

PETER RUSSELL

Library of Congress Control Number: 2017917308

ISBN: 978-1-928586-13-5

Published by Elf Rock Productions,
2375 E Tropicana Ave, 8-273, Las Vegas, NV 89119-8329

Contents

Rediscovering the Timeless Wisdom

W E LIVE IN unprecedented times. Science is answering age-old questions about the nature of reality, the birth of the cosmos, and the origins of life. We are witnessing technological advances that a century ago would have seemed science fiction, or even magic. And, more alarmingly, we are becoming increasingly aware of the impact that our burgeoning growth is having on the planet. Yet, along with these rapidly unfolding changes is another development that's passing largely unnoticed. We are in the midst of a widespread spiritual renaissance, rediscovering in contemporary terms the timeless wisdom of the ages.

Most spiritual traditions began with a person having some transforming mystical experience, a profound revelation, or clear inner awakening. It may have come through dedicated spiritual practice, deep devotion, facing a hard challenge, or sometimes simply unbidden, out of the blue—a timeless moment in which one's personal dramas pale in the light of a deep inner peace and sense of fulfillment. However it came, it usually led to a delightful joy in being alive, an unconditional love for all beings, and the dissolving of a sense of personal self.

The profound transformation they experienced led many of them to want to share their discoveries, and help others have their own awakening. But those who listened to their teachings may have misunderstood some aspects, forgot others, and perhaps added interpretations of their own. Much like the party game Chinese whispers in which a message whispered round a room can end up nothing like the original, as the teaching passed from one person to another, from one culture to another, and was translated from one language to another, it gradually became less and less like the original. The timeless wisdom became increasingly veiled, and clothed in the beliefs and values of the society in which it found itself, resulting in a diversity of faiths whose common essence is often hard to detect.

Today however, we are in the midst of a spiritual renaissance that differs significantly from those of the past. We are no longer limited to the faith of our particular culture; we have access to many wisdom traditions, from the dawn of recorded history to the present day. Moreover, the insights of contemporary teachers from around the planet are readily available in books, audio recordings, videos, and on the Internet. None of this was possible before.

Rather than there being a single leader, there are now many experiencing and expounding the perennial philosophy. Some may be more visible than others, and some may have clearer realizations than others, but all are contributing to a growing rediscovery of the timeless wisdom. We are seeing through the apparent differences of the world's faiths, past their various cultural trappings and interpretations, to what lies at their heart. Instead of the truth becoming progressively diluted and veiled as it is passed on, today our discoveries are reinforcing each other. We are collectively honing in on the essential teaching.

As we strip away the layers of accumulated obscurity, the core message not only becomes increasingly clear; it gets simpler and simpler. And the path becomes easier and easier.

There is a growing recognition that awareness of our true nature does not need studious reading of spiritual texts, years of meditation practice, or deep devotion to a teacher; only the willingness to engage in a rigorously honest investigation into the nature of awareness itself. Not an intellectual investigation, but a personal inquiry into who and what we truly are.

The Easiest of Times;
The Hardest of Times

Buddha had it easy. He was not distracted by television, the Internet, news of disasters in foreign lands, or the latest shenanigans of stars and politicians. He did not need to return phone calls, respond to the emails piling up in his inbox, or catch up with the latest tweets and Facebook postings. He did not have to work at a job in order to pay the bills. He was not worried by stock market crashes, radiation leaks, climate change, or bank failures. His mind was not ceaselessly buzzing with the dull roar of traffic, muzak, and an ever-present electrical hum. He was not bombarded by seductive advertisements telling him he lacked this or that and could not be happy until he had them. He was not embedded in a culture that sought at every turn to engross his attention in unnecessary thoughts and distractions.

Yet his path was hard. The only spiritual advice he had as a young man was from traditional Vedic priests who advocated elaborate rituals and sacrifices as the path to salvation. He had to leave home and spend years wandering through the forests and villages of northern India searching for spiritual guides. And those of any help were few and far between; the spiritual pioneers of the time were just beginning to realize that spiritual liberation came from within rather than a deity of some kind. He tried everything available, studying with the best teachers he could find, even adopting austerity to the point where he nearly died of starvation. But, in the end he had to work it out for himself. When he did he came to the then radical realization that it is our clinging to our ideas of how things should be that cause suffering, and keeps us apart from our true nature.

Today we have it so much easier. We can reap the benefit of Buddha's discoveries—and those of his followers who added their own realizations. We can learn from the wealth of other Indian philosophies that have evolved over the centuries, and from Taoist teachings, Sufis, Western mystics, native wisdoms and other traditions. Not only do we have the benefit of centuries of spiritual enquiry in so many cultures, we can also access the wisdom of the many awakened people alive today. We can go sit at their feet, read their words, listen to recordings, watch videos or live streams on the Internet. We also have advances in psychology, neuroscience, chemistry and biology to augment our understanding and experience. Most significantly, we are distilling the diverse expressions of this perennial wisdom into a common understanding. Stripping away the trappings of time and culture, we are collectively discovering that the essence of awakening is simply letting go of our preconceptions and judgments, returning our attention to the present moment, and there recognizing our true nature.

In short, on the one hand, it is becoming easier and easier to awaken; on the other hand the times we live in make it ever-more challenging. How do they balance out? Overall, is it any easier or any harder than 2,500 years ago? Who is to say? But we can shift the balance in our favor by taking advantage of the growing wealth of wisdom that is now so readily available, choosing the most effective and direct paths to awakening. Yet being ever mindful of the distractions of our contemporary world that make it so challenging to stay awake.

Returning
to Natural Mind

Behind all our endeavors lies the desire to feel good—to be happy, feel content, relaxed, and at ease. No one wants to be in pain or to suffer unnecessarily. This is our true bottom line. We may think we are seeking some external goal, but we are seeking it in the hope that, in one way or another, we'll feel better for it.

Why then, are we so seldom at peace? After all, we're intelligent beings, who can look ahead and plan for the future. Moreover, we have many tools and technologies with which to create a better world. One would think that we, of all creatures, would be content and at ease. Yet the very opposite seems to be true. Our pet dog or cat seems to be at ease much more of the time than we are.

Paradoxically, it is our remarkable ability to change the world that has led us to this sorry state. We have fallen into the belief that if we are not at peace, then we must do something about it. We believe we need to attain some goal, possess some thing, find some new experience; or conversely, avoid a situation or person that is causing us distress. We assume that, if we could just get our world to be the way we want it to be, we could finally be happy.

In the short term, this approach seems to work. When we get what we want, we usually do feel better. But only for a while. Before long, we are off in search of some other source of happiness.

We live in what Indian philosophies call *samsara*, which means "to wander on endlessly." We wander on, looking for happiness in a world that provides but temporary respites from our discontent, fleeting satisfactions followed by more wandering on in search of that ever-elusive goal.

Ironically, believing that peace of mind comes from what we have or do often results in the very opposite. The idea that something is missing or needs changing creates a sense of discontent. Our attention becomes preoccupied with what we need, the choices to be made, the plans to carry them out—much of it concerning situations that don't yet exist, and probably never will. Our thoughts move from one issue to another with seldom a pause.

Throughout history, there have been those who've discovered a timeless truth about human consciousness: our natural state of mind is already one of ease and contentment. By "natural" they do not mean the state of mind in which we spend most of our time—which, for the vast majority, is not one of ease and contentment. They are speaking of the mind before it becomes tarnished with worries and concerns. It is how we feel when everything is OK; when we are not worrying about anything.

Time and again they've told us that we don't need to do anything, or go anywhere to return to this natural state of ease. We simply need to let go of any attachments as to how things should or should not be; become aware of our experience in the present as it is, without resistance or judgment. Then—and this is key—let the attention soften and relax.

When we do, we taste how it feels to be free from worry, anticipation and planning. We find the peace of mind that we have been seeking all along. A peace that is not at the mercy of events, or the vacillations of the thinking mind. A peace we can return to again and again.

EFFORTLESS MEDITATION

Y OU MAY BE surprised to hear that meditation should be effortless, that no striving or concentration is needed. I know I was. When I first became interested in meditation, I was repeatedly told that it took great mental discipline and many years of practice. Indian teachers had likened the mind to a wagonload of restless monkeys that needed to be tied down and kept quiet.

And my experience appeared to confirm it. My mind was full of thoughts, and try as I may, I could not keep them at bay. Like many others, I naturally assumed that I was not trying hard enough; I needed greater mental discipline, not less.

Then I chanced upon Transcendental Meditation. Its teacher, the Maharishi of Beatles fame, challenged the whole notion of trying to control the mind. The monkeys, he pointed out, were wanting something—more bananas perhaps. Give them what they want and they will settle down of their own accord. So with the mind; it is restless because we are seeking something. And what is it we are seeking? We want to feel better--to be happier, more at ease, content. He argued that if we give the mind a taste of the inner contentment it is looking for, it will be attracted to it and begin to settle down of its own accord.

This made more sense to me than what I'd come across so far, so I learned his practice. And it worked. I found my mind becoming quiet without any effort. Indeed, as soon as I inadvertently started trying to control the process, in the hope that I could somehow help my meditation along, it did not work so well.

Now I am not suggesting that this applies to every type of meditation. Techniques designed to cultivate particular mental skills or states of mind, may well involve a degree of concentration or mental discipline. But when it comes to the basic skill of relaxing into a quieter state of mind, effort generally turns out to be counter-productive.

Instead, when you realize you have been caught in a thought, accept the fact. Don't judge or blame yourself. It happens—even to the most experienced meditators.

Instead of following the thought, as you might in normal life, gently shift your attention back to your experience in the present moment. And just notice what is there. It may be sounds around you, sensations in the body, the breath, some feeling, a sense of ease or peacefulness. It doesn't matter.

Let the attention rest in the experience. Don't try to concentrate or hold it there. Ah yes, you will be sure to wander off again. But the practice is not learning how to stay present, but learning how to return to the present. If you wander off a hundred times, that is a hundred opportunities to practice gently returning your attention to the present.

Even then, trying and effort can arise in subtle ways. Maybe if I just added this or focused on that, it would be easier. Some of it is so subtle that we don't even notice we are doing it. A slight attempt to control the mind, a faint resistance to an experience, even wanting to have a good meditation, they all stand in the way of our letting go completely.

But when we do, we discover that there really is nowhere to get to, and nothing to do. It was the doing that was holding us back.

NOT RESISTING RESISTANCE

THE BUILDING WHERE I used to run a meditation group was on the same street as a fire station. One could almost guarantee that sometime during the meditation a fire engine would come rushing past, sirens wailing. Not surprisingly, people would afterwards complain. "How could I meditate with that noise?"

How often have we felt something similar? There's an unspoken assumption that the mind can only become quiet if the world around is quiet. We imagine the ideal meditation setting to be somewhere far from the madding crowd—a retreat deep in a forest, a peaceful chapel, or perhaps the quiet of one's own bedroom. It is much harder for the mind to settle down in a noisy environment.

Or is it?

I suggested to the group that the next time a fire engine came blasting by they look within and explore whether the sound really was that disturbing? After the following meditation, a woman reported how the noise no longer seemed a problem. It was there, but it didn't disturb her. The disturbance, she realized, came not from the sound itself, but from her wishing it weren't there.

This was the essence of Buddha's realization 2,500 years ago. We all experience what he called *dukkha*, conventionally translated as "suffering." In Pali, the language of Buddha's time, *dukkha* is the negation of the word *sukha*, meaning "at ease." So *dukkha* might also be translated as not-at-ease, or discontent—an experience we all can relate to.

The root meanings of these words add further insight. *Sukha* stems from *su* (good)-*kha* (hole), and generally referred to a good axle hole in the wheel of a cart. The wheel was a great technological boon of the time, and whether or not it ran smoothly around its axle would have been a primary concern for both comfort and efficiency. Conversely, the root of *dukkha* is *duh* (bad)-*kha* (hole). There is resistance to the smooth running of the wheel, leading to friction and discomfort.

Similarly with the mind. When we accept things as they are, "go with the flow," there is ease—*sukha*. This is our natural state of mind—content and relaxed. *Dukkha*, suffering, arises when we resist our experience. Our natural state of ease becomes veiled by a self-created discontent.

Thus, as numerous teachers have pointed out, we can return to a more peaceful state of mind by letting go of our attachments as to how things ought to be, and accepting our experience as it is. Not wishing for something different, not creating unnecessary discontent.

Upon hearing this, people often ask: Does this mean I should accept injustice and cruelty, the homeless sleeping on the streets, or the recalcitrant attitude of my partner? Of course not. There are numerous situations that we should not tolerate, and each of us, in our own way, will be called to do what we can to improve things.

"Accepting our experience as it is," means just that; accepting our experience in the moment. If you're feeling frustrated, angry, or indignant, accept the feeling. Don't resist it, or wish it weren't there; but let it in, become interested in how it feels.

We can also explore the feeling of resistance itself. It can be quite subtle, and not easily noticed at first. I find it useful to simply pause and ask: "Is there any sense of resistance that I am not noticing?" Then gently wait. Some resentment or aversion towards my experience may become apparent, or sometimes a faint sense of tension or contraction in my being. Then, rather than focusing on the particular experience that I'm resisting, I turn my attention to the felt sense of the resistance itself, opening to this aspect of "what is."

Rather than my experience being divided into two parts—the actual experience in the moment, and my resistance to it—the feeling of resistance is now included as part of the present moment. As I allow the resistance in, it starts to soften and dissolve. Then I can be more open to whatever it is that I was resisting. I can allow it in, and begin to accept the experience as it is.

So when you find something seeming to disturb your inner peace—whether it be a friend's behavior, some politician on TV, or a passing fire engine—pause and notice what is happening inside. See if there is any sense of resistance to your experience. If so, open up to the experience of resisting. Be curious as to what is going on and how it feels.

By not resisting the resistance, but accepting it as part of "what is", you will probably discover that you can be at ease in situations where before you would have suffered.

WAITING IS

"Waiting Is"—a phrase immortalized in Robert Heinlein's celebrated sci-fi novel *Stranger in a Strange Land*.

For most of us waiting is not easy, often a bore. Waiting for a bus or plane, we look for something to do to pass the time. Sitting in a doctor's waiting room, we idle away the minutes thumbing through magazines of no particular interest. Alternatively we check our email, social media or the newsfeed, not wanting to waste time.

We want the waiting to be over with, so that we can get on with the more important things we need to do.

On the other hand, simply waiting—not waiting for any event to happen, just waiting without wanting—can be an enlightening experience.

The mind relaxes, and there is space for more of the present to reveal itself. We begin to notice aspects of our world that we weren't aware of before— the sound of the refrigerator or a distant conversation, a tree gently waving in the breeze, the smell of cooking, or some feeling in the body. It doesn't matter what; and it will probably be different every time.

The practice of just waiting need not wait until we find ourselves waiting for a bus or sitting in a "waiting room." Any moment of the day we can choose to pause for a while and simply wait.

Waiting without any concerns about what may be next. It doesn't matter. Waiting is.

Start right now. Pause. Take a breath. Relax... and wait...

The Parable of the Rope

WE ARE LIKE a person holding on to a piece of rope. He holds on for dear life, knowing that if he let go he would surely fall. His parents, his teachers, and many others have told him this is so. As he looks around he sees everyone else is holding on tightly. Nothing would induce him to let go.

Along comes a wise person. She knows that holding on doesn't work, that the security it offers is illusory, and that it only keeps you where you are. So she looks for a way to dispel his illusions and help him set him free.

She talks of a deeper joy, of true happiness, of peace of mind. She tells him that he can taste this if he will just re-lease one finger from the rope.

"One finger," thinks the man; "that's not too much to risk for a taste of bliss." So he agrees to take this first initiation.

And he does indeed taste more joy, happiness, and peace of mind.

But not enough to bring lasting fulfillment.

"Even greater joy, happiness and peace can be yours," she says, "if you will just release a second finger."

"This," he tells himself, "is going to be more difficult. Will I be safe? Do I have the courage?"

He hesitates, then, flexing a finger, he feels how it would be to let go a little more… and takes the risk.

He is relieved to find he does not fall; instead he discovers a greater happiness and inner peace.

But could more be possible?

"Trust me," she says. "Have I failed you so far? I know your fears, I know what your mind is telling you—that this is crazy, that it goes against everything you have ever learned—but please, trust me. I promise you will be safe, and will know even greater happiness and contentment."

"Do I really want inner peace so much," he wonders, "that I am prepared to risk all that I hold dear? In principle, yes; but can I be sure that I will be safe, that I will not fall?" With a little coaxing he begins to look at his fears, to consider their basis, and to explore what it is he really wants. Slowly he feels his fingers soften and relax. He knows he can do it. He knows he must do it. It is only a matter of time until his grip releases.

And as it does an even greater sense of peace flows through him.

He is now hanging by one finger. Reason tells him he should have fallen a finger or two ago, but he hasn't. "Is there something wrong with holding on itself?" he asks himself. "Have I been wrong all the time?"

"This one is up to you," she says. "I can help you no further. Just remember that all your fears are groundless."

Trusting his quiet inner voice, he gradually releases the last finger.

And nothing happens.

He stays exactly where he is.

Then he realizes why. He has been standing on the ground all along.

And as he looks upon the ever-present ground, he finds true peace of mind.

Retire

Retire
No, not at the end of your working life, when you finally retire from earning a living and take more time for yourself. Retire now, in everyday life.

Let the mind retire.

Let your attention step back from whatever may be occupying your mind. Become aware of what was already there, before the thought caught hold.

Maybe there's an emotion, a feeling, some sensations in the body, your breath, sounds around you. It doesn't matter what it is. Different things become apparent at different times. Just notice whatever is already there, but had passed unnoticed.

Then retire again. Let the attention step back to become aware of what is there, beneath the sensations and feelings.

Again, there is no right answer. It is the process itself that is valuable. Just pause and notice what is there.

And then, retire again.

And again...

Loving Your Self

Love your self. It's a common refrain. One understanding of this is loving who you are — accepting yourself just as you are, warts and all; having compassion for your shortfalls, while rejoicing in your gifts. Loving ourselves in this way is certainly valuable; it can lighten our self-judgment and self-criticism, and free us to live more authentically.

Another way in which we can love ourselves is to take that feeling of love that dwells in our hearts, the feeling we know when we love someone, and let it flow towards ourselves — not loving anything in particular about ourselves, simply experiencing love for ourselves.

And there is another, deeper quality of self, often called the "pure" or "inner" self, or simply "the Self." It is that ever-present sense of "I." This inner feeling of "I-ness" that never changes. It is the same feeling that was there yesterday, last year, and as far back as we can remember. Our thoughts, our likes and dislikes, our personality, desires, and beliefs may have changed considerably over the years, but the "I" that experiences them all has not.

It is the "I" in "I am." The "I" that is aware. The "I" that is knowing this moment right now, that knows every experience we've ever had or ever will have.

Most of the time we don't notice this quiet inner sense of being. Our attention is on what we are experiencing. But when our attention relaxes and we become aware of that which is experiencing all this, we find an inner peace and ease, a great contentment to which nothing needs be added. We have come home.

Knowing our essential being is divine. Mystics have written volumes on it. Enlightened ones have urged us to open ourselves to it, and soak in the calm and joy it brings.

To rest in the Self is so delicious we cannot help but love it.

It is what we've been longing for.

It is the beloved.

You are The Beloved.

THE SELF DOES NOT
IDENTIFY WITH ANYTHING

IT IS SOMETIMES said that the Self identifies itself with the ego, with thinking, or with the body. This is effectively saying that the "I" that is aware believes itself to be a separate self—a thinker, a chooser, a doer of actions.

But the pure Self, does not believe or think anything. It is that which is aware of the thoughts and beliefs that are arising—the "knower" of all this.

Rather than the Self identifying with an experience, it is that our attention becomes absorbed in the experience.

Attention can be thought of as the spotlight of awareness, focusing on one particular aspect of the breadth of the totality of our experience. Its job is to focus on things that may be important.

The attention has two basic modes of operation. The first is a relaxed mode where everything is OK. We are at ease, and the attention moves effortlessly, from one possible interest to another, with no voluntary effort or control—attracted to the sound of a bird, an itch, a moth flying by.

Then when we do notice something of interest our attention stays there for a while. We pay attention. Is this something I should be concerned about? Do I need to do anything? If so what? The focus of our awareness is now on the issue at hand, and the thoughts we are having about it.

When the issue at hand seems important for our well-being, the seamless whole of our experience is divided in two. There is "me", the organism that needs to be taken care of, and there is the world around that may need to be changed in some way—or conversely be prevented from changing. A sense of being an individual self arises. It identifies itself with the body, and believes it is one who is thinking and acting in the world. However, as you begin to explore this sense of a separate self, you discover that it is just a set of thoughts and beliefs. It is another experience arising in awareness.

It is like a character in a novel. If the novel is engrossing, we, the reader, can become so absorbed in the story, the ups and downs of the hero's adventure, that we temporarily forget we are the reader of the story. Our attention is absorbed by the drama. Similarly with the dramas of our own lives, our attention becomes absorbed in our own hero's journey—the challenges and opportunities, our hopes and fears, the tasks facing us, the choices we must make, the risks we must take.

In our thinking there is an identification with the character in our personal story. But the pure Self, the knower of all experience, has not identified with anything. It remains, as ever, the silent witness of all these shenanigans. It is simply aware of them as it would be of any other thought or experience.

So when we say we have become identified with the ego, with our thoughts or the body, what is actually happening is that the attention has become so absorbed by these aspects of our experience that they dominate our reality. For a while, the fact that we are much more than that does not get a chance to enter. We get lost in the plot again, and forget we are that which is watching the drama unfold.

Praying to Self

W<small>E USUALLY THINK</small> of prayer as an appeal to some higher power. We might pray for someone's healing, for success in some venture, for a better life, or for guidance on some challenging issue. Behind such prayers is the belief that we don't have the power to change things ourselves—if we did, we would simply get on with the task—so we beseech a higher power to intervene on our behalf.

But what is it really that needs to be changed? Mostly we seek to change the world in order to create the circumstances that we think will make us happy—or conversely, avoid those that will make us suffer. We believe that if only things were different we would finally be at peace. However, when we look more closely at why we are not at peace, we may find that the root of our discontent lies not so much in the situation at hand, but more in how we interpret it.

If I am stuck in a traffic jam, I can see it either as something that will make me suffer in some way—being late for an appointment, missing some experience, or upsetting someone—and so begin to feel anxious, impatient or frustrated. Alternatively, I can see it as an opportunity to relax, and take it easy for a few minutes. The same situation; two very opposite reactions. Yet the difference is purely in how I am seeing things.

When I catch myself feeling upset in some way, I find it helpful to remember that my annoyance might be coming from the way I am interpreting the situation. If so, it makes more sense to ask, not for a change in the world, but for a change in my perception.

So that is what I pray for. I settle into a quiet state, then ask, with an attitude of innocent curiosity: "Could there, perhaps, be another way of seeing this?" I don't try to answer the question myself; to do so would doubtless activate the thinking-mind, which loves to try and work things out for me. So I simply pose the question. Let it go. And wait.

Often a new way of seeing then dawns on me. It does not come as a verbal answer, but as an actual shift in perception. I find myself seeing the situation in a new way.

One memorable shift happened a while ago when I was having some challenges with my then partner. She was not behaving the way I thought she should. (How many of us have not felt that at times?) After a couple of days of strained relationship, I decided to pray in this way, just gently inquiring if there might possibly be another way of perceiving this.

Almost immediately, I found myself seeing her in a very different light. Here was another human being, with her own history and her own needs, struggling to navigate a difficult situation. Suddenly everything changed. I felt compassion for her rather than animosity, understanding rather than judgment. I realized that for the last two days I had been out of love; but now the love had returned.

The results of praying like this never ceases to impress me. I find my fears and grievances dropping away. In their place is a sense of ease. Whoever or whatever was troubling me, I now see through more loving and compassionate eyes.

Moreover, the new perspective often seems so obvious: Why hadn't I seen this before?

The beauty of this approach is that I am not praying for intervention in the world, but for intervention in my mind, for that's where help is needed most.

Nor am I praying to some external power. I am praying to my self for guidance—to the inner Self that sees things as they are without the overlay of my hopes and fears. It recognizes when I have become caught in the ego's way of thinking, and is ever-willing to help set me free.

FORGIVENESS

FORGIVENESS DOESN'T ALWAYS seem easy. If we feel attacked or hurt, we may feel that the only way to relieve our pain is to attack back in some way. We want others to know how much we're hurting. At such times forgiving them may seem far from our minds.

Forgiving someone can also feel like we are backing down or letting them off, implying "I know you did wrong, but I'm not going to punish you this time."

But true spiritual forgiveness is far from just saying "I'm letting you off." It can actually be a profound healing, especially for the person who is feeling hurt.

In the bible the Greek word that's translated as "forgive" is *aphesis*. Its literal meaning is "to let go" — as when we let go of a rope, or something else we are holding on to. We're releasing our grip on something. With forgiveness, the grip that we're releasing is a mental one. We're letting go of the judgments and grievances we are holding against a person, and our beliefs about how they should have behaved.

When someone doesn't behave as we have expected, or as we would have liked them to, we tend to feel angry. And when we do, it's easy to think that the other person has made us angry. We hold them responsible for our feelings.

But when we look more closely, we usually find that our discomfort is coming, not from their actual behavior, but from how we've interpreted it—the story we are telling ourselves about what they've done, what we're accusing them of, and how they could have behaved better.

One thing that can help is to put ourselves in the other person's position. If we could truly understand their motives—what they were thinking and feeling, their fears and pains, their own background and conditioning—all the influences in their life, that have led them to this point in time—then we might begin to understand why they did what they did. We can begin to see them through the eyes of compassion rather than judgment.

We can begin to recognize that although they may not have behaved as we believe they should have done, they were in a sense behaving exactly as they should have done—given all the past situations and influences that led up to this.

True forgiveness comes when we recognize that deep down the other person was wanting exactly what we are wanting. In their own way they were seeking to be more at peace, to ease their own suffering. But the way they set about doing this conflicted with our own ideas as to how to be at peace.

This is not to imply we should simply accept their behavior, or even condone it. We may well feel the need to give them feedback or make suggestions as to how they might behave better, but let us do so from a compassionate heart rather than a judgmental mind.

KINDNESS

After 45 years of research & study, the best advice I can give is to be a little kinder.

—Aldous Huxley

THE WORD "KIND" stems from "kin"—those of the same family or tribe, those we are close to, those of the same kind.

Deep down we are all of the same kind. We all want to feel at ease, to be treated with respect, to feel cared for and appreciated. None of us want to feel criticized, rejected, humiliated, ignored or manipulated. To reduce it to its simplest terms, we each want to feel loved. I do not mean love in a romantic sense, or some outpouring of emotion, but simple caring. This is the universal bottom line of every human relationship. We all want to feel cared for. We want to be treated kindly.

If each of us would like to be treated with kindness, then it should be our intent to give this to others. But often we do the exact opposite. Instead of trying to ensure that the other person feels cared for and appreciated, we can end up in a vicious circle of recrimination and attack.

It usually starts with feeling hurt over something that someone said or did. Whether they intended to hurt us, or whether it is only in our imagination, doesn't matter. The fact is we feel hurt. Then, if we are not fully conscious of our own inner processes, we are likely to defend ourselves by attacking back in some way. It's not the noblest or wisest response, nevertheless that is the way we less-than-enlightened folk tend to react.

It may be a cutting remark or criticism, a resentful tone of voice, a shift in body language, or simply a prolonged silence. Whatever form it may take, the underlying intention is that the other person should feel just a little hurt—not much, not enough to disrupt the relationship, but sufficient that the other person should not feel totally loved.

But if the other person is also less than enlightened, their response to a perceived attack will likely be similar to ours. They will tend to attack back, doing or saying something intended to make us feel just a little hurt and not totally loved.

Soon a vicious circle gets set up. It may not always be that obvious. On the surface it often looks as if the relationship is going well; both people appear friendly with no open hostility. But underneath a sad game is being played out. Each person, in their attempts to have the other person behave in a more loving manner, is actually withholding love. They're effectively saying to each other: "You're not respecting me, therefore I'm going to be unkind to you so that you realize the error of your ways and treat me better."

It's a lose-lose game. Little wonder then that many relationships—personal, social, or work—find themselves on rocky ground

The vicious circle can be broken if we start from recognizing that just as we want to feel loved and at ease, so do they. Our intention then becomes: How can I communicate so that the other person does not feel attacked or rejected, but cared for and respected?

We can start by becoming vigilant against attacking attitudes. Filtering out our less-than-noble thoughts can remove much of the problem at source.

This does not mean we should not speak our truth. Instead, explore how to do so in a way that the other person feels appreciated rather than attacked. When you have something difficult to say, you might preface it with the reason why you want to say it, letting the person know it comes from an attitude of caring rather than attack. For example, you might start by saying: "I value our relationship, and want to see it grow, but for that to happen, I need to discuss an issue that is difficult for me." This sets a very different tone than simply blurting it out.

Or it may help to express your own fears—they are also part of the truth. Revealing your fear of rejection or of being misunderstood, can help others appreciate your concerns and put them more at ease—which, remember, is the goal of this exercise.

And when this practice slips, as it surely will from time to time, and the attacking mode creeps back in, there is nothing like a genuine apology to set things back on track. Own up to your mistake (we are all human after all), and try to express yourself again with a more caring intention.

This practice of kindness is essentially *The Golden Rule* found at the heart of the world's spiritual traditions. In the Bible it is said: "All things whatsoever that ye would that men should do to you, do ye even so to them." Similarly, in the Koran we find, "No one of you is a believer until he desires for his brother that which he desires for himself."

If we all applied this to everyone we met or spoke to, the world would be a very different place.

THE SUPPORT OF NATURE

B ACK IN THE sixties, I spent time studying Transcendental Meditation with Maharishi Mahesh Yogi at his ash-
ram in Rishikesh, India. When he was assessing how we
were each progressing in our practice, he was usually not
so interested in our experiences within meditation itself—
such as whether we were having deep insights or visions,
or tasting higher states of consciousness. His principal interest was whether we were noticing, what he called, "in-
creased support of nature." By this he meant: Were we noticing that the world seems to support our needs and inten-
tions—what many of us today would call synchronicities,
or meaningful coincidences.

He reasoned as follows: In meditation we are transcending, that is "going beyond," the thinking mind. Much of our
thinking is concerned with our personal needs and desires.
And many of the problems we see in the world—from inter-
national and environmental problems to social and personal
problems—stem, in one way or another, from our self-cen-
tered thinking. Thus, in transcending this way of thinking,

we are freeing ourselves from a root cause of our problems, and are therefore supporting nature in the most fundamental way possible.

And nature returns the favour by supporting us!

I have never heard of any other teacher taking this approach (which is not to say there may not be some). And although it may sound a little like "magical thinking," I have noticed it to be frequently true in my own life. When I am meditating regularly, and especially when I have been on a meditation retreat, life seems to work out very well, many little coincidences leading me to just what I need at that time. On the other hand when I'm stressed, not in touch with my inner being, but caught up in my needs and wants, synchronicities like this do not flow so well.

Where Are You?

To the question "Who are you?" we may answer, the "I" that is aware, the knower of all experience.

When are you? "Now" is the obvious answer. "I" am always in the present moment, even though my thoughts may be about the past or the future.

Where are you? "Here" you might say. Where else?

But what do you mean by *here*? You'd probably point to the particular place in the world where your body happens to be. And it is easy to assume that this is also where your consciousness is located.

Right now these words probably appear a foot or two in front of you. Further in front of you may be a table; there is the ground beneath you; and perhaps through a window some more distant scene. The world appears arrayed around you—around the "I" that is aware of it all—somewhere in the head.

The feeling that our consciousness is somewhere in our head seems to fit with the fact that our brains are also in our heads, and brains are somehow associated with conscious experience. We would find it strange if the brain was in the head, but you felt your self to be in the knees.

But all is not as it seems. The apparent location of your consciousness does not actually have anything to do with the placement of your brain. It depends on the placement of your senses.

Your primary spatial senses—your eyes and ears—happen to be located on the head. Thus the central point of your perception—the point from which you seem to be experiencing the world—is somewhere behind your eyes and between your ears—somewhere, that is, in the middle of your head. The fact that your brain is also in your head is just a coincidence, as the following thought experiment bears out.

Imagine, that your eyes and ears were transplanted to your knees, so that you now saw and heard the world from this new vantage point. Where would you now experience your self to be? In your head? Or down by your knees? Your brain may still be in your head, but not the central point of your perception. You would be looking out onto the world from a different vantage point. Placing your self at the center of this new view you would indeed feel your self to be somewhere around the knees.

Today this need not remain a thought experiment. With virtual reality it is possible to create a phenomenon called *telepresence*, literally, "distant presence." A virtual reality headset is fed information coming from cameras and microphones placed around a dummy head in another room. For a person wearing the headset their primary spatial information is now coming from the other room. Within a few minutes they begin to feel themselves to be located in the other room.

In short, the impression that your consciousness is located in space is an illusion. When you come to locate your sense of self, you quite naturally imagine yourself to be at the center of your perceived world. But the whole of your perceived world is a representation of reality appearing within you. It is not that you are someplace in the world. The truth is just the opposite. Everything you perceive is within you.

Consciousness cannot be located anywhere within the world of your experience; it is that within which this world appears.

RIPPLES OF KNOWING

WHAT ARE THOUGHTS made of? They are not material things; they are not made of atoms or anything physical. Yet our thoughts clearly exist. What, then, is their essential substance?

Because we don't often consider this question we don't have any ready words for the "stuff" from which mental phenomena are made. Perhaps the best we can say is they are made from mind-stuff. That doesn't in itself say much, except to emphasize that they are not made of matter-stuff.

One might say that the stuff of the mind is consciousness. But some caution is needed here. The word "consciousness" has various meanings and my idea of it may be different from yours.

In addition it is a noun, which implies it is some "thing." And is therefore something that can be known in some way, however subtle—another object of knowing, rather than that which knows all experiences.

The word "conscious" derives from the Latin *conscius*—literally, "with knowing." The suffix "ness" in conscious-ness means "the state or quality of." It is appended to an adjective to create an abstract noun that allows us to talk about that quality in a general way. Happiness is the state of being happy. Softness is the quality of being soft. But neither happiness nor softness exists as an independent "thing". Similarly there is no such "thing" as consciousness. The word refers to "the state or quality of" being conscious—of being "with knowing."

So one could say the common essence of all thoughts is the knowing of them. They are made of knowing.

An analogy is often drawn with waves in water. A wave is just water in motion. It does not exist as an independent entity, separate from the water. It is merely the way the movement is perceived.

Similarly, our thoughts are ripples of knowing, which are experienced as words in my mind, with perhaps some image from the past and maybe an associated feeling. But the thought has no independent existence beyond my knowing of it. It is but a temporary ripple in the ever-present field of knowing.

The same is true of any other experience that may appear in the mind. The images that constitute a memory are all "in the mind," and are likewise just modulations of the field of knowing. So too are the scenes we experience when we imagine the future.

It is only a short step to appreciate that the same applies to our experience of the material world. If you close your eyes and explore your experience of your body, you will find various sensations—some pressure in places, some warmth here, a tingling there, or some tension perhaps. These too are but ripples in the field of knowing. The different sensations become integrated into the experience of having a body. But, like the various sensations, this experience of a body is another modulation of the field of knowing.

Similarly with sound. It is easy to appreciate this when we imagine some music. That clearly is an experience arising in the mind. There is no essential difference with "live" music. The brain is taking the data relayed to it from the ears, and from that creating the sound of music. This is experienced as coming from an external world beyond the body, but that experience is itself still arising in me, another excitation of the field of knowing.

As information from other senses is added in, our mental representation of the world begins to take on the mantle of an independent reality. We begin to believe that the world arising in our awareness *is* the world out there—the so-called "real" world.

This is made all the more convincing as soon as we open our eyes.

Vision takes us out into the world of an apparent external space that seems to be independently real and filled with material objects. But however much it may appear so, we are forced to accept that the visual experiences themselves are also just ripples of knowing.

This is where it begins to get mind-bending. We may realize that the colors we experience are just appearing in the mind—the light itself is not colored, it is simply energy of varying frequencies, the color we experience coming from the representation of that frequency in the mind—but it is more difficult to appreciate the same is true of the solidity we experience around us. It not only looks solid, we can touch it, feel its solidity, and experience how it impedes our movement. We seem to be experiencing the world directly, but in truth all that we are experiencing, including its apparent solidity, is a representation of the world "out there" appearing in our field of knowing. It is how the information that the senses detect appears in the mind.

We can explore this representation in the mind, and from that draw conclusions about the nature of the physical world—which is what science aims to do—but all that we discover, all that we know and understand about the world, all our scientific theories and mathematical equations, our concepts of matter, energy, space and time, our notions of quarks, strings, particles and waves, are but appearances in the mind, more ripples in the field of knowing.

It is all knowing, knowing ripples of knowing. Knowing knowing itself.

PETER RUSSELL

Peter Russell is a leading thinker on consciousness and contemporary spirituality. He is the author of nine other books, including *The Global Brain*, *Waking Up in Time* and *From Science to God*.

Peter believes that the critical challenge today is to free human thinking from the limited beliefs and attitudes that lie behind so many of our problems—personal, social, and global. His mission is to distill the essential wisdom on human consciousness found in the world's various spiritual traditions, and to disseminate their teachings on self-liberation in contemporary and compelling ways.

He has a rich website, *The Spirit Of Now* (www.peter-russell.com), containing numerous articles, recordings, videos and meditations.